Two Little F Words

by Christina Acevedo, Red Seal Chef, RHN

Honey and Vanilla

Christina Acevedo
Two Little F Words

First Edition

ISBN 978-1-7773994-2-9

Jacket Design and Layout by Marina Hawkeswood of Mainstay Communications.

For those who are diabetic or have thyroid imbalances, once you start eating lower carb you may instantly have to lower your medication. Consult your doctor before you start including TRE into your lifestyle.

The entire contents of this publication are based upon the opinions of Chef Christina Acevedo. Please note Chef Christina Acevedo is not a dietitian, physician, pharmacist or other licensed healthcare professional. The information in this book is NOT intended as medical advice, nor is it intended to replace the care of a qualified health care professional.

The content is not intended to diagnose or treat any diseases. Always consult with your primary care physician or licensed healthcare provider for all diagnosis and treatment of any diseases or conditions, for medications or medical advice as well as before changing your health care regimen.

Contact Christina via www.HoneyandVanilla.com/contact

This book is dedicated to my mom.

You have consciously and unconsciously

given me the gift of unconditional

love and self-responsibility.

And a special thanks to E for encouraging me to speak

my truth and share my story.

Contents

Introduction

Have you found that over the years, you have less energy than you did before? A cloudy brain at times? Aches and pains you can't figure out the source of? Most people just say, oh you are just getting old! If you ask me, the "getting old" excuse is the thing that is "getting old". I believe the reason we get those aches and pains and feel more tired than we did in our younger years is because of two things: we have accumulated too many toxins over the years and we have lost our wholeness; or the synergy between our mind and body.

In order to get our wholeness back we must begin with one of the fundamental ways of achieving optimal health: nourishing our bodies with whole food. There are many pillars involved in maintaining optimal health such as proper sleep, looking inward with some form of meditation, reducing EMF exposure, increasing sunlight exposure and including different forms of detoxification protocols. But for the purpose of this book and for our attention spans, I want to focus on one of my favourites, well, two of my favourites, the power of Time Restricted Eating (TRE) and how to nourish our cells and mind with food.

One of the main objectives of this book is about bringing awareness to the detrimental effects of consuming a diet high in refined carbohydrates and the impact they have on our overall health. The information that is contained in this book is simple and understandable and will change your life forever if you apply it.

Food and nutrition are an entry point to bringing awareness into your life, but that awareness does not have to stop there. Once you start eating consciously, making food prep a weekly priority and you understand the power whole foods have on your mind and body, you will naturally want to create more wholeness in your life and pay more attention to other pillars of optimal health such as quality sleep, exercise and daily detox. Allow the knowledge in this book to awaken your awareness to a life that can be lived optimally in whatever stage you are at.

What I am about to propose to you is not a diet. However, I believe many diets such as ketogenic, carnivore, and paleo all have their benefits in certain moments of one's life, as they can help rebalance the body. Instead, what I am proposing is a lifestyle. From my personal experience of practicing TRE and eating optimally throughout the days, months and years, I have become more WHOLE. I feel like this lifestyle is an achievable goal to attain and not one that makes you feel like you have failed once it's over. It just becomes part of your every day life, like brushing your teeth.

I hope this book will help you understand how important it is to rethink what healthy food actually is, what a personal health plan is, and how you can begin to change your conditioned thoughts. I feel society teaches us to numb ourselves with food, TV, drugs, smoking etc. instead of helping us to look within ourselves for answers. As of this moment, the top five chronic diseases in the world can all be correlated, if not caused solely by, the "food" that we consume.

So let's take a deeper look at our optimal health, but here is a warning: there will be some swearing involved, it's good for the soul.

Oh Snap!

It's possible to live a long healthy life into your 80s 90s and 100s. We can grow old and empower our vitality within. It's time to take control of our lives and live with whole intentions!

My Story

I grew up off the island of Montreal, Quebec in a little town called Chateauguay, with the best cook in the world: my mom. I would literally call her from school to ask her what we were having for dinner. Our diet consisted mainly of vegetables, meat, starchy carbohydrates and grains. When I look back on our diet in those younger years I still feel we ate fairly well growing up in the 80s and 90s with the knowledge we had. We rarely had processed food in our house and my mom even made our school lunches. True fact, in high school I got an award for "The Weirdest Lunches" and when I look back on why I received that award, I think it was because I was the only one that didn't buy lunch from the school cafeteria. Of course, living in Quebec, French fries and poutine were staples (but not weekly ones). Vive la poutine!!!

After finishing high school in 1995, I went on to receive my Red Seal as a professional French Cuisine Chef in 2000. I then moved to Calgary, Alberta, to pursue my education as a Registered Holistic Nutritionist™ and received my certification in 2006. I continue to advance my knowledge by attending conferences in the latest science and research in Functional Medicine.

With all of the education I've completed I created my own business, Honey and Vanilla. Through the years it has grown many branches, which forms the holistic approach I help people apply to their lives. I've worked as a personal chef, cooking for clients on a weekly basis, and created workshops on specific ailments such as: "The Origin of Alzheimer's disease", "The Importance of Sleep and Why We Do It" and "The Pillars of Optimal Health". I also educate the public on the benefits of fasting and provide one-on-one nutritional consultations.

I believe the food we choose to eat, the way we choose to think and the energy we choose to be around has the power to balance (or imbalance) our WHOLE body and mind.

Every chapter of my life has been an opportunistic lesson. However, when I was younger, I chose to ignore those lessons and refrain from growing as a human being. The older I get, the more I recognize the gifts I am given each and every time a new chapter in my life is being presented to me. The last five years or so have been quite a challenging time, it has been a choice to either see the light in a very torturous dark chapter or to follow that darkness and continue the programmed cycle. I'll explain what I mean by this a little later.

After my mom cared for her mother who suffered for many years with Alzheimer's disease, my grandmother passed away peacefully in her hospital room with her two daughters by her side. I had no idea of the physical and mental stress my mom went through in those days while caring for my grandmother, as my sister and I were young women trying to find our purpose in life. I don't remember supporting my mother through those times or asking her questions about how she felt or how the whole experience impacted her life. I didn't know two thirds of Alzheimer's patients are women and that someone is diagnosed with the disease every three seconds.[1]

Oh Snap!

"We are dying of 21st century diseases
because we are still practicing 20th century medicine."

- Dr. Dale Bredesen

I do recall one significant moment. Years after my grandmother passed away, my mom and I were remembering things my grandmother used to do and how they impacted my mom's present behaviour and in turn how they impact my present behaviours, AKA a programmed mind. My mom never really explained in detail what she went through with my grandmother and her struggles with Alzheimer's but she did tell me with a very serious tone that she would consider taking her own life if she ever got Alzheimer's disease. At the time I didn't know how serious she was.

In 2015, we were sitting in my mom's doctor's office and were told my mom had MCI (mild cognitive impairment), the beginning stages of Alzheimer's disease. In the conventional way of thinking, this was the beginning of the end for my mom. There was no hope—she would lose her memories of the life she had built with my dad. All I could think about was the life they had worked so hard to enjoy and how they were just starting a new chapter of their lives: retirement.

Oh Snap!

It is time to take back what has always been ours, our bodies and our minds. No more excuses or blaming our genes. In order to achieve optimal health we must take responsibility for ourselves and not rely on others to do it for us. The best part is that it can just start with one thing, such as daily time restricted eating.

If you could just switch the balance of consuming refined foods to consuming more whole foods and eat less often you would save more money, eat less, have a lower medical bill, have more energy and a longer, healthier life span.

I also recalled that conversation we'd had so long before and as we stood in the parking lot of her doctor's office, holding each other, both of us crying, I told her that whatever she needed me to do, I would do it, no questions. I just wanted the unknown and the pain to go away. I now see that at that moment the universe was giving me a gift to now be able to nurture my mom and be there for her just like she has always been there for me.

Since this chapter in my life has started I've found myself crying regularly for two reasons: I feel so bad for my mom and dad—she doesn't deserve this nor does he—and I've been crying for something I could not understand for the longest time: the loss of my relationship with my mom when she hasn't even left this physical world. The dynamics have changed; the comfort I would yearn for from my mother whenever I was going through something hard is no longer an option. This pains me deeply every day, but I have had to learn to wean myself from this deep dependant comfort I always had with her and find it from within, from myself.

Whenever I felt bad, sad, sick or unsteady, I would go see my mom and she comforted me. Usually that feeling gets taken away from you when your mom passes away but when someone has Alzheimer's you mourn that nurturing relationship while they are still alive because you become the caregiver, if you choose to.

After my mom was diagnosed with MCI, my beliefs on nutrition and food were upgraded. I started to read and research as much as possible on how to eliminate this imbalance in her body, but I felt defeated. All of the conventional research said that it is a progressive disease, there is no hope and to prepare for the worst. People even encouraged me to just accept it and come to peace with what was happening. Surrender.

Well, if you know me, you probably know what I said: fuck that! (I promise that's the only F-bomb in this book.) My mom needed more than what conventional medicine knew. She needed a "think outside the box" approach. She needed a thought process that understood the root cause of this imbalance and that process came from my love for holistic living, seeing the body as an energetic being and applying a functional medicine approach. I now understand that Alzheimer's disease is not a disease at all, it is just a symptom of many possible underlying root causes, as are all other chronic diseases.

After watching many documentaries and reading many research papers and books, I became very fascinated with the latest research coming from Dr. Bredesen. According to him, there are more than 36 possible biomarkers (factors) that will trigger brain "downsizing" and prevent re-growth. He presents these theories in his book: The End of Alzheimer's. The factors that can lead to different forms of dementia include blood sugar imbalance, insulin resistance, lack of growth factors, mitochondrial dysfunction and toxicity through heavy metals or mold. All of these biomarkers create inflammation in the body and imbalance the soul.

When thinking of the many possible causes of dementia, I considered the fact that our brain is made up of 60% fat, mostly in the form of cholesterol and DHA (docosahexaenoic acid). It made me realize that our present diet, which is high in refined carbohydrates and low in fat was the worst possible food plan she and anyone else could be following.

Doctor Bresden's research, published in 2014 on Reversal of Cognitive Decline, showed that among many therapeutic components of his program, a diet low in simple/refined carbohydrates was implemented to many of his patients with significant positive results.[2]

After reflecting on everything I was doing for my mom, this journey made me realize I had another lesson to learn: how to take care of myself going forward. I am half my mother—both through her DNA and programmed mind. So it is up to me to express those genes through thought and lifestyle choices. I realized my own wholeness was not optimal. I needed to improve my overall diet and lifestyle, not only to attain optimal health but also to prevent Alzheimer's for myself. Alzheimer's runs in our family and through the knowledge I learned, I realized that diet and lifestyle could make a huge difference in my health destiny.[3]

At first I put myself into ketosis along with my mom, which is when the body has depleted its glucose storage from the liver and starts using fat in the form of ketones as its main source of fuel. I felt amazing. I felt lighter, clear headed and energetic. But something in me felt out of balance—I felt like I was being too strict. I did not realize that being in ketosis 24/7 was not the best plan for many women. I now know that it is important for me to carb it up with quality carbohydrates a week before my menstrual cycle begins and to just take a more balanced approach.

So I listened to my body and I chose to eliminate most of my refined foods (that included my monthly boxed organic mac and cheese), implement different forms of fasting such as FMD (Fasting Mimicking Diet), daily TRE and to consume mostly whole foods: vegetables, fat and protein also known as "VFP". Plus at times I need a little gluten-free grain here and there to please Mable (my other personality who expresses herself a couple of days a month). Ladies, you know who I mean.

I know, you are probably thinking: that's what a nutritionist should be doing anyway! Well, even nutritionists fall into slumps of bad eating habits and convince themselves it's fine. After introducing an updated version of my nourishment plan (VFP + TRE and honouring my circadian rhythm), I could not believe the difference in how I felt. I do not feel bloated anymore, my weight is consistent, my head is clearer (most of the time) and I have a lot more energy. I have noticed a remarkable difference in my stage four endometriosis and feel empowered to continue learning how to live optimally.

After creating a new food plan for my mom and I, the enormous power of whole food and fasting screamed out to me, urging me to share my super simple recipes and formula on how to nourish the body. **Through torturous enlightenment, Two Little F Words was born.**

CHAPTER ONE

Whole Foods

"

When a flower doesn't bloom, you fix the environment in which it grows, not the flower.

- Alexander den Heijer

It's understandable that you may think living optimally takes so much work and is expensive and difficult to achieve, but I'm here to tell you it can be really simple. When I changed my food plan I was so annoyed I couldn't eat bread anymore and that I was now the obnoxious person at a restaurant who asks how much sugar is in something or what type of flour is used. Ugh, I was annoying. I was only annoying until I stopped caring what other people thought, I do this for myself and if people roll their eyes I must reflect the mirror onto them. Oh Shit!!!

My recommendation is to just start with a few simple holistic tools such as fasting for longer daily, eating more vegetables, quality fat and quality protein (VFP) all in the form of real whole food!

We all have different definitions of what a healthy food plan actually is and it changes as our knowledge increases and we become aware of what our body is asking from us. My idea of healthy eating has changed during my career as a Holistic Nutritionist. Eating a sandwich on whole wheat bread used to be my definition of healthy eating until I started to ask more questions, attended functional medicine conferences and listened to how my body felt when I ate something.

Eating optimally for your health is not just about eating the right whole foods, you need to have a whole awareness behind your decisions. In order to receive the most nutrients and energy from your food, pay attention to the following:

- How is the food prepared? High heat, bad oils, aluminum or non-stick pans?
- What is the quality of your whole foods, is it organic, non-gmo, seasonal or local?
- How does your body and mind feel daily with the food you consume? Bloated, tired?
- How often do you eat? Are you really hungry or just bored?
- Where and how did your food get on your table? Mass production or small local farms?
- How much packaging and what type of material was used to wrap up the food you purchased?

I understand not all of the above guidelines can be accomplished by everyone, I don't always check them all off. There are many variables when it comes to trying to eat better, such as income, lack of cooking skills, time, where you live etc. But I still don't believe that any variable is a valid excuse for not increasing your optimal health. Just by choosing to focus on one of the above with the whole food and time restricted eating concept in mind, you are creating new energy and empowering yourself to do better. If you feel you cannot find or afford quality whole food then TRE is part of your golden ticket to optimal health. True fact, in many studies it has been shown that when mice and people eat the exact same food (glucose) in a daily restricted time frame, they can balance their metabolic markers much quicker than if they were to eat all day. In other words, its not just about what you eat but the time when you eat.

Let's just be clear that when I say 'eat whole foods', you don't get a thumbs up from me just for shopping at a giant chain organic grocery store that has the word WHOLE in it. Yes, they do sell real whole foods, but unfortunately some large grocery chains who promote themselves as "whole" have really done a disservice to the meaning of what whole foods are.

These big corporations have manipulated our brains to think whole foods can come with nutrition labels that say "natural" and "healthy" even when they are filled with food colouring, preservatives and are packaged in plastic bags and boxes not regulated by our governments. WTF?

Think of eating whole foods as completing a full circle of life. We raise animals, use their meat to nourish our bodies and use their manure to nourish our soil in order to grow nutrient-dense fruits and vegetables. We pick the fruits and vegetables, consume them to fuel our bodies and use their scraps to nourish our compost in order to create rich, nutrient-dense soil. It is one of nature's most beautiful and cooperative processes.

Oh Snap!

Don't be fooled by claims of "whole wheat" being better for your blood sugar balance. Yes, whole wheat does release glucose slower, but in the end your insulin is still being activated constantly if you are eating whole wheat bread on a regular basis because even whole wheat bread eventually gets broken down into its simplest form: glucose. Same goes for gluten- free bread, it's no better in regards to insulin resistance.

A Word On Accumulation

When people say "I ate it growing up and I'm fine" they don't consider how invisible toxins accumulated in their bodies. As a result, they pass these bad eating habits on to their children. We need to understand the word 'accumulation' in order to achieve optimal health and feel whole. Over the years, the accumulation of toxins from our food, our minds and our environment have created the weaknesses within our bodies, making room for disease. In other words, accumulation of toxins (thoughts, food and outer sources) without supporting our detoxification system creates disease. Our detoxification system (liver, kidneys, lungs, mind and skin) and immune system can only handle so much over the years, and if we do not practice proper detox protocols day after day, year after year, the toxins in our body and mind will accumulate to the point where our systems are overworked and can no longer function optimally. This leads to losing our wholeness. Understanding this is Prevention 101.

Dr. Tom O'Bryan's research on toxic accumulation has woken me up. His findings point out everything from chemicals sprayed on food crops to BPA leaching from coffee cup lids into coffee is having a harmful effect on life across the planet. For example, babies are being born with high levels of toxic accumulation, there is an ever increasing drastic and irreversible loss of vertebrae life around the world, highly reduced sperm count in men and disrupted estrogen production in women.[4]

CHAPTER TWO

Understanding Carbohydrates

"

In the soil of ignorance, fear can easily be sown.

- Heather Brooke

The word carbohydrate means different things to different people and it has been misunderstood and wrongly categorized for a long time due to the influence of our governments and the corporate world. We were never guided towards choosing the nutrient dense forms of carbohydrates (vegetables) or taught how they improve our health.

The 2015-2020 Dietary Guidelines for Americans clearly states the overall rate of infectious diseases has dropped but the rate of chronic, diet-related diseases has risen. This is clearly a red flag when the American government's guidelines state how half of the American population have one or more preventable diet-related chronic diseases. This kind of information blows my mind! [5]

Refined and Processed Carbohydrates

(Those which deplete the body)

Oh Snap!

I want you to understand how refined sugar sources do not just come from consuming cakes, cookies and soda. They come from "healthy" granola bars and cereals, flavoured yogurt, store bought condiments, refined grains such as rice, pasta and bread. This correlation is desperately needed in order to start making better choices. Dopamine is one of our neurotransmitters that brings us joy and makes us feel like we are on top of the world. Studies on rats have shown that if you give them sugar or cocaine as a choice of food, they will choose sugar.

Refined carbohydrates are literally addictive to the brain because they activate a part of the brain (the amygdala) associated with reward, cravings and addiction.[6]

Refined carbohydrates deplete the body of its wholeness for many reasons. I believe the biggest reason is because we have been told to consume most of our food from this 'grain' category, so we end up over consuming them. Excess creates imbalance. This overconsumption of simple forms of carbohydrates, such as white bread and granola bars which rapidly release energy, can lead to many imbalances in the body such as insulin resistance, weight gain, high blood pressure, high cholesterol, Alzheimer's, and Type 2 Diabetes.

People who consume refined foods or refined carbohydrates as their primary source of energy feel the need to eat every two to three hours, are often called grazers, and easily get "hangry" as people say. I was one of them. Refined carbohydrates do not satiate you for a long period of time because they lack the synergistic properties needed to increase long-lasting satiation. This is one of the reasons why you feel the need to eat every two to three hours. Your body is like, yo, I need my crack (sugar) intake stat or i'm gonna flip out!

"If you crave sugar or carbohydrates after a meal, have trouble going more than four to five hours without eating, have high triglycerides, or are overweight (particularly in the midsection), you are likely a "sugar-burner". This means that your metabolism is looking for more sugar to fuel your energy and cellular function rather than tapping into the vast resource of stored energy in your fat cells." Dr. Brian Mowll, *The Blood Sugar Manifesto.*

According to the World Health Organization (WHO) in 2013, the average person was consuming 63 grams of free/added sugar a day in their diet. In 2019 the WHO recommended consuming less than six teaspoons, or 25 grams, of free sugar/added sugar a day (this does not include the natural sugar you would get from whole fruits and vegetables). To give you a realistic picture of how easy it is to consume over 26 grams of added sugar a day, the average "healthy"vanilla yogurt has 33 grams of sugar in 1 cup and the food industry portrays yogurt as a healthy choice.[7 8]

Unrefined Carbohydrates (Those which nourish the body)

Unrefined carbohydrates have not been violated, unlike their mistreated twin I just discussed. Since unrefined carbohydrates have not been refined or stripped of their essential nutrients that make them whole, they can be super nourishing to the body and soul. They are filled with the sugars, starches, fibre, minerals and vitamins that feed our cells and make us whole.

Unrefined carbohydrates have the amazing nutritional properties your body needs to thrive. I believe, as do many of our leading experts, our every day food intake should consist mostly of unrefined carbohydrates, especially in the form of vegetables. Yes, vegetables are a good source of carbohydrates! Below are examples of unrefined carbohydrates:

Whole Fruits

Nuts and Seeds

Whole Grains* (I personally feel overconsumption of grains whether whole or refined lead to health issues and should be eaten in small quantities if tolerated)

Dried Legumes

Whole Vegetables

Do you see how much simpler it is to explain refined versus unrefined carbohydrates? In keeping with the "excess creates imbalance" theme, if we consume most of our carbohydrates from starchy carbohydrates, legumes, whole grains and fruits, I believe the body will react the same way it would as when we eat refined carbohydrates because in excess, they can spike our insulin which can lead to insulin resistance and imbalance our health.* As Dr. Jason Fung says, "the dose makes the poison." This is why I believe it is important to limit the amount of starchy carbohydrates, grains, fruits and legumes we consume in order to keep your cells insulin sensitive. Keeping our cells insulin sensitive helps keep our blood sugars in balance which in turn reduces the risk of many chronic diseases.

In 2016, The American Journal of Clinical Nutrition studied 38 males and found that a diet high in saturated fat and low in refined sugar didn't cause heart disease. It led to reduced fat storage in the liver and heart and reduced triglycerides.

Also, it is important to note the 1977 dietary guidelines (which recommended people eat mostly refined carbohydrates) were never tested to see if these recommendations were safe. The Canadian Food Guide used to recommend canola oil and soybean oil as a good source of fat. These oils are usually highly refined and cause overall systemic inflammation in the body AND many are subsidized by our government! [10]

Can I put a thought in your head to ponder for a moment? Have you ever considered that maybe the diet we have been told to eat (high grain consumption) for the last 60 years is making us fat and sick?

Most of our beef cattle are raised on grain for a certain amount of time in their short lives. Why? Because it's cheap, grain is subsidized by the government, and it fattens them up quickly. So, if we as a society consume mostly refined carbohydrates in the form of grains/bread/pasta/cereal because they are cheap, they fatten us up and they are subsidized by the government, don't you think our governments are kind of treating us just like conventional cows?

Too many refined carbohydrates such as grains make cows fat and sick and they make us fat and sick too. Crazy, right? As the great philospher Hippocrates explained, "Everything in excess is opposed to nature."

CHAPTER THREE

The Profitable Betrayal of Refined Carbohydrate

"

It's All About the Benjamins Baby.

- Puff Daddy

When I started looking into what foods were causing the most harm to our bodies I thought for sure it would be what our governments and scientists were saying all along: fat! After researching the newest science from a functional medicine standpoint and seeing many of the scientific papers published in the last five years or so, it was quickly evident excess refined carbohydrates and low fat diets were killing us, all of us, and not slowly.

Let's ask a crazy question: how do refined carbohydrates (sugars) influence laws and regulations?

In 2003, George Bush's Secretary of Health and Human Resources, Tommy Thompson, flew to Geneva and told the WHO that if they publish their report on limiting daily sugar requirements, they would no longer receive funding from the U.S government. [11]

Let me give you a little history on the last 60 years of the supposedly healthy food guidelines our governments have told us to follow. The story goes like this: eat less fat and consume more refined carbohydrates because they are good for you. We have not done any scientific research to ensure this is the healthy way to go, and yes, we do subsidize grains and dairy - but trust us, we have your best interests in mind and not in our wallets. Cheeky right?

In the 1950s, a physiologist named Ancel Keys studied the influence of diet on our health. Since fat has more than twice as many calories as protein and carbs, Keys assumed high cholesterol causes heart disease and saturated fat increases cholesterol. Or in other words, the devil was fat and refined carbohydrates were good. (This information is documented in many books such as *Eat Fat, Get Thin* by Dr. Mark Hyman.)

Due to Ancel's influence for the past 50 to 60 years, we have been told to think fat is bad for us, especially saturated fat, and to consume less fat and more refined carbohydrates in the forms of wheat, soy and corn. In 1977, the American government published a food guide that encouraged society, and in turn the majority of the population in North America, to consume more and more of their energy from refined carbohydrates—at least six to eight servings of refined carbohydrates a day from bread, cereal and pasta, and to continue consuming low fat products. Here is another way of looking at it: according to our experts, over 50% of our diet should come from three different plants: soy, wheat and corn. Does that feel balanced to you?

If we reflect on the last 60 years, what has happened to us since we let go of our traditional way of eating large amounts of whole foods and started eating more refined and processed foods ? We are fatter, have more type two diabetes, depression, atherosclerosis, Alzheimer's, anxiety and metabolic syndrome than ever before.

According to the WHO, the world has seen a steady increase in heart disease, diabetes, dementia and cancer. The WHO concludes most of the conditions are **preventable**, and that dietary changes are just one of the crucial tools that need to be implemented in order to have a healthier lifestyle. [12]

The correlation between dietary fat, specifically saturated fat and heart disease, has been disproven over and over again in the past decade. In Julia Reedy's 2016 thesis on *How the American Low Fat Recommendations Contributed to Health Decline*, she explains how the quality of the fat we eat and the way it is constructed is what defines a good quality fat. If you want to nerd out, read her thesis.

When looking at the updated 2019 Canadian Food Guide, it no longer seems to recommend specific types of unsaturated fats to consume. They do recommend eating less than 10% of your daily fat intake from saturated fat but they do not give healthy examples of unsaturated fats to consume. Unrefined, organic cold pressed extra virgin olive oil, avocados, raw nuts and seeds are all great sources of quality fats to consume daily.

Summary of All the

Good Shit

You Have Learned in Chapters 1to 3

- The overconsumption of refined carbohydrates depletes the body of essential nutrients and increases chronic disease.
- One of the best holistic tools you can use to achieve optimal health is to eat more WHOLE foods and less refined foods.
- The dose makes the poison.
- Quality fat does not make us fat, excess sugar such as refined carbohydrates do.
- Vegetables are a form of carbohydrate, we want to eat this form of carbohydrates the most to achieve optimal health.
- Peanut butter sandwiches, granola bars and "real"juice boxes are all a source of refined carbohydrates and excess sugar.
- Excess refined carbohydrate consumption leads to increased hunger and wanting to graze all day.
- We must detox our body and minds daily to avoid accumulation and in turn decrease the chance of chronic disease.

CHAPTER FOUR

Fast and Feast

"

The biggest challenge you are going to have to face in your life is you.

- Les Brown

Fast

The idea of not eating as often throughout the day and condensing our eating window into a smaller amount of time is quite stressful for many. Nowadays people on average consume food for 15 hours a day, thus never giving the body any time to truly rest, digest, detox and repair.

THE best thing I have ever included in my holistic tool kit is Time Restricted Eating (TRE) daily. It gives the body time to clean itself up on the inside without having other energy-sucking tasks to do like digesting your food. It lowers your insulin levels and allows the body to become more efficient in burning glucose and burning fat for energy once you become metabolically flexible. This means you can switch from burning glucose to burning ketones for energy more efficiently.

"

The best of all medicines is resting and fasting.

- Benjamin Franklin

In general, we are a society of excess and tend to have concern for our health only when something bad happens. We are not taught to pay attention to the little imbalances and signals our body gives us before the imbalances become too big, we are taught to blame our genes and not take responsibility for our choices. It is time to stop this useless way of thinking, and TRE is a great way to get control back.

My daily fasting times change throughout the year, according to the season and how I am feeling - but I am never eating more than fasting. At the moment I fast 16 hours daily, I do not eat from 6 or 7 pm till 10 or 11 am the next day with the exception of a black coffee in the AM. Adding cream or sugar to your morning coffee will break your fast, so drink it black or don't drink it at all until you have broken your fast. For some people black coffee raises their blood sugar levels, you may want to do some experimenting.

I occasionally do a 24 hour fast, maybe twice a month to really do some house cleaning, and a couple of times a year I partake in a longer fast such as three day water fasts or the five day fasting mimicking diet by Prolon.

One of the worst pieces of advice I have ever given my clients in the past —and that we received from our scientific community and food guides—is to eat five to six times a day. This advice is not backed up by science and really doesn't respect how the human body works on an evolutionary or circadian rhythm level. Our bodies are designed to fast and feast in order to balance our whole system, especially to balance our insulin levels. This is why I am so passionate about implementing daily time restricted eating. [13,14]

I used to say this all of the time: "Oh no, I have to eat every two to three hours or else my blood sugar will go too low and I'll feel hangry". Little did I know my hypoglycemia was due to insulin resistance. After implementing the powerful tool of TRE (of course I had hunger pains at first) I quickly realized my conditioned mind had the power and that I wanted the power back, so I trained my body to eat less often throughout the day and turned my cells into insulin sensitive heroes.

If you can relate to being "hangry", this means your body is addicted to the constant surge of glucose you are giving it every two to three hours, and because you are possibly consuming mostly refined carbohydrates. Once I put my clients on a time restricted eating/whole food plan the first thing they say to me is, "I can't believe I am not hungry all of the time."

One of the biggest lessons I have learned through my mom's illness has been to take responsibility for my own health. Bringing my wholeness back or attaining optimal health is about prevention; it is about empowering myself to take control of my health and not blame my genes for every health condition I have. In order to change my perception on health I learned I must become the awareness behind my conditioned mind and take responsibility.

Most of the time when we think we are hungry, the feeling is actually something else we do not want to deal with, such as boredom, habit, discomfort, sadness, anxiety, fear. All of these emotions drive us to eat more than we should.

Once I started being more aware of why I ate and when I ate, I realized there were emotions connected to those cravings. Now I give in less. I take control of my mind and take responsibility for my emotions and most of the time, my emotions or ego don't win. **How can we possibly take our mind and health back into our control if we cannot control our thoughts?**

BENEFITS OF FASTING

1. Lowers insulin levels and blood sugar
2. Activates stem cells (after three days)
3. Activates autophagy (some say after 13 hrs)
4. Reduces inflammation
5. Increases health span and longevity
6. Balances cholesterol levels
7. Reduces the risk of cardiovascular disease
8. Increases ketone levels
9. Increases weight loss
10. Increases mental clarity
11. Improves gut health + balances gut microbiome
12. Increases the health of your immune system
13. Can help balance your circadian rhythm
14. Reduces the risk of Alzheimer's Disease

Benefits are activated depending on the type of fasting and length of time you fast.

HOW TO START TRE &
MAKE IT PART OF YOUR LIFESTYLE

1. Start with nourishing 12 hours a day and fasting for 12.

2. After a week, increase your fasting by an hour, feast 11 fast 13.

3. Try to get to feast 10 fast 14 or feast for 8 fast for 16.

4. When you nourish, choose VFP (veggies, fat, protein).

5. Eat two nutrient dense meals a day with a snack in between if needed.

6. Do not eat 2-3 hours before bed. That's it!!

Note: It's much easier to fast longer if you can reduce your refined carbohydrates and increase your good fats. Remember this timeframe is not set in stone, we are cyclic beings. Try different hours and see what works for you.

Feast

So you may be asking yourself, what do I feast on when I decide to nourish my body with food? The answer is quite simple, eat real, quality forms of whole veggies, fat and protein, also known as VFP.

Most of the time I try to base my food needs according to my sleep, my stress levels, what is available locally and seasonally, plus the weather and my cycle, just to name a few. This allows me to look from within; it allows me to connect to myself and really understand what is best for me that day, that week, that hour.

I believe what is most important to remember when applying this kind of lifestyle (eating less often and fasting for longer throughout the day) is to be sure that when you do eat you NOURISH and not just fill yourself up.

To give you an idea of what I would eat in a day, it goes something like this;

- 12oz water with raw apple cider vinegar first thing in the morning.
- Black coffee.
- First meal at about 11am: chia pudding with blueberries and seeds, an avocado, four or five olives, two eggs and homemade seedy gluten-free bread.
- Second meal at about 5pm: big-ass salad with homemade dressing, sausages, roasted sweet potato fries and a homemade chocolate banana muffin.
- At times there is a snack at about 3pm that consists of veggies and dip, an apple and raw milk cheese.
- When we focus on nourishing our bodies and minds with TRE and VFP there is no need to count calories, read food labels or worry. Your body has an easier chance of becoming metabolically flexible.

I encourage all of you to look into to TRE and other forms of fasting and implement them into your lifestyle. It is now proven and well known that in order to achieve and maintain optimal health it is imperative to include some form of fasting into your health protocol.[15] Two great resources for the science behind the benefits of fasting are Dr. Mindy Pelz (especially for women) and Dr. Valter Longo, who's book *The Longevity Diet* recommends the FMD (fasting mimicking diet).

CHAPTER FIVE

Embrace the Change Yo

"

We can't change the world unless we change ourselves.

- Biggie Smalls

There is going to be an adjustment period when you reduce refined carbohydrate intake and begin fasting for longer throughout the day. At first, your taste buds will be in shock and you may want to throw my super yummy vegan chocolate banana muffins in the garbage because you will think they are bad because there is no added crack (sugar) in them. You may feel kind of tired, constipated, have low energy, crazy cravings or want to kill your significant other. This is due to your body saying goodbye to relying on so much glucose and toxins and hello to more overall quality nutrients, less food and more fat burning. But, with that said, you may not feel any discomfort, so think positive vibes yo!

Psychologically, your ego can feel threatened, it can manifest as feeling more anxious, irritated, angry, sad and depressed. Dr. Joel Furhman explained the process of detoxification brilliantly at the 2018 Addiction Summit: "Many times feeling bad (not terrible) is getting better and feeling good is getting worse. Because when you feed the addiction you are stopping the process of detoxification and breakdown of toxins. When you start emptying the body of toxins you are going to feel bad."

You want to support the system when detoxification begins. If you are feeling really terrible, can't sleep, can't go to work and feel nauseous, (which I don't think you will feel if you start slowly with 12/12) I believe you are doing more harm than good. It means your elimination organs are not ready for that much toxic dump and that you are just recirculating the toxins. You need to support your detoxifying organs in order to properly eliminate. You can do this by increasing your fibre, slow down on the daily TRE, stay in the 12/12 range for a bit longer if needed, drink water, eat lots of cruciferous vegetables such as cabbage and cauliflower. You can also take certain supplements such as milk thistle that support the liver, plus you can allow your body to sweat that shit out by taking saunas, dry brushing and exercising.

If you just feel kind of irritated, maybe low energy, want to kill your significant other, or have a mild headache, I would celebrate that and realize your body is starting to clean itself from the inside out. Shit ya!

I thought it would be a good idea to share my daily routine so you can get an idea of how you want to create your own plan. When I sat down and started to create my daily practice and routine I acknowledged the following:

My Daily Routine

- What am I looking to achieve? For me it's Alzheimer's prevention, increase my health span and reduce my symptoms from endometriosis.
- What are the weak spots in my body? My liver, detox pathways, gut and reproductive organs.

How much time every day do I want to commit to my health goals? Two to three hours. Then I created my plan and researched the best possible holistic and functional medicine tools to help get me to my optimal self. Please note, these change according to season and what I feel my body and mind needs.

- Own my morning by waking up between 5:30 and 6am.
- Have a large glass of water with raw apple cider vinegar.
- Make a delicious, comforting black coffee (no cream, nada).
- Then I sit and read a book for an hour while my sauna heats up, check my email and social media (sigh), then I take a sauna and practice gratitude and affirmations or watch Netflix while I sweat my butt off!
- I then shower and start my day by serving others and cooking amazing nutrient dense whole food.

- I break my fast at 10 or 11am and stop eating at 6 or 7pm.
- I use only natural cleaning products and essentials oils.
- I sit with myself and become aware of my thoughts and visualize.
- I implement a quality sleep routine.
- I eat mostly organic, local, seasonal whole foods.
- I am sure to have a daily bowel movement.
- I sweat in my sauna three to five times a week.
- I am sure to get out in nature daily, get my heart pounding (the hardest thing for me).
- I exercise (even just walk) daily for thirty minutes or more.
- I do strength training twice a week (this hasn't happened yet).
- I dry brush or use a rebounder to get my lymphatic system going.
- I practice daily breathing such as WimHof method.
- I also take certain supplements to optimize my liver and optimize drainage pathways within my body.

By creating my own livable and achievable daily routine with the above holistic tools, I am able to be consistent and disciplined with my practice. I also plan a weekly food menu for my husband and I according to weather, how we are feeling, how busy we are, if my menstrual cycle is about to start, what's in season, what's on sale, etc.

I assure you after a while you will feel a new sense of comfort and joy with this transition. As Bruce Lee once said, "A conditioned mind is never a free mind." Free the conditioned mind and you will feel free.

Summary of All the

Good Shit

You Have Learned in Chapters 4 to 5

- Always fast longer throughout the day than feasting.
- Free your mind by taking back the control, do not let your ego take you over.
- Think of how you can detox your body and mind daily with simple things.
- Create YOUR own daily optimal health routine, own your morning and set the energy for the day!
- Prevention is KEY to optimal health and health span.
- Embrace discomfort. Uncomfortableness is when you grow the most as a human.
- Eating frequently throughout the day never gives your body a chance to heal itself.
- Break your daily fast with good sources of fat such as avocado, olive oil, olives, nuts.
- Check in with yourself and ask why you are wanting to eat, are you really hungry?

CHAPTER SIX

The Goods

"

Recipes are like a river, they are
never the same one moment to the next.

- Jacques Pèpin

So here it is, the first of many books. My love, whole intention and offering to you. It was really hard to pick which recipes made the cut but this is just the beginning, and this is my calling: to nourish, nurture and share the knowledge I have learned through my own experiences and from others.

These recipes were created from my past and present experience with my mom having Alzheimer's and trying to find delicious alternative recipes to meals my mom and I used to love. They come from thoughtful intention of keeping things simple, reducing insulin and blood sugar levels, reducing overall inflammation, increasing optimal health and reducing the risk of chronic disease. Most importantly they taste delicious, they are not hard to make, and many of them freeze well or keep in the fridge for days.

This is not a therapeutic diet such as when people go into ketosis for certain types of chronic diseases like Alzheimer's. Eating real whole foods and implementing time restricted eating is a lifestyle, there is no need to count calories when you cut your eating window down and you are eating mostly whole foods.

Please note the following recipes are all gluten-free, organic, mostly grain-free, some dairy-free, and some vegan. I use only sweeteners from raw honey, maple syrup or ones naturally occurring in the fruit I choose. If you cannot use all organic ingredients, check out the dirty dozen from EWG.com to choose which products are most important to buy organic. I always recommend you buy organic meats, dairy and oils.

Breads, Buns and Crackers
Soups
Salads and Dressings
Mains
Dips and Sauces
Snacks
A Bit of Real Sweetness

Bon Appétit!

Recipes

Breads, Buns + Crackers

I have chosen to go gluten-free 98% of the time due to Dr. Alessio Fasano and many others' work on how gluten affects the gut lining and can increase inflammation in the body. I feel a huge difference since removing gluten from my diet and will continue to do so as a preventative measure. When I removed gluten from my diet many years ago and then had my mom go gluten-free, I had to find delicious alternatives. It was definitely a disaster at first but through patience and many experiments I found some pearls. I can't wait for you to find your favourites in the following recipes.

Tia's Dilly Almond Buns

GLUTEN FREE + GRAIN FREE | YIELD 6–10 BUNS

TIA'S BUNS ARE A CLASSIC recipe to have around the house all year round. They freeze super well and you can whip them up in no time. You can turn these babies into savoury treats with jalapeños and cheese or add some sweetness with cinnamon, raisins and maple syrup. The choices are endless.

INGREDIENTS

2 cups almond flour
1 tbsp flax meal
1 tbsp aluminum free baking powder
½ tsp sea salt
⅓ cup organic grass-fed sour cream
2 eggs
3 tbsp olive oil
2 tbsp fresh dill or chives (1 tbsp dried)

METHOD

1. Preheat oven to 325° Farenheit.

2. Whisk the wet ingredients in one bowl and mix the dry ingredients in another bowl. Fold the wet ingredients into the dry. You can use muffin pans to get the perfect shape or you can make six large drops or 10 mini-sized drops using a spoon or small ice cream scoop onto a baking sheet lined with parchment paper.

3. Bake 10-15 minutes or so, check after 10 minutes. If a skewer comes out clean, they are ready.

Note: These buns freeze really well, so you can double the recipe. I really like to make mini burgers and sandwiches out of these jewels. They are a little more delicate but just be gentle when picking up your super yummy burger or sandwich.

Vegan Rosemary Almond Buns

GLUTEN FREE, GRAIN FREE + VEGAN | YIELD 8–10 BISCUITS

I HAD MY SECOND PROUDEST moment in recipe creation when I came up with these buns. They are moist, super flavourful and are delicious with poached eggs. Don't tell your fussy guests they are gluten free and vegan as they will have no idea, I promise.

INGREDIENTS

3 tbsp ground flax seeds
5 tbsp water
1½ tsp freshly chopped rosemary
1 tsp garlic powder
1 tbsp aluminum-free baking powder
½ tsp salt
1 tbsp psyllium husk
2 cups almond flour
3 tbsps olive oil
½ cup full fat coconut mylk

METHOD

1. Preheat oven to 325° Fahrenheit.

2. Combine your flax "egg" mixture in a small bowl and let stand in fridge for 5-10 minutes.

3. In a large bowl add all of your dry ingredients and in a smaller bowl the coconut mylk and olive oil. When your flax "egg" is ready, add it to your wet ingredients.

4. Combine your wet to your dry ingredients and fold together with a rubber spatula. Divide the mixture into 8-10 dollops on a baking sheet lined with parchment paper. Bake for 20-25 minutes and allow to cool slightly before removing. Store in fridge or freezer.

Crispy Nut + Seed Crackers

GLUTEN FREE, GRAIN FREE + VEGAN | YIELD 24 CRACKERS

WHEN I CAME ACROSS THE original version of these crackers I was blown away by how easy and tasty these were. I have added a little bit more flavour to these babies and I think it really kicked them up a notch. The trick is to make them nice and thin, so use the correct size baking sheet or split the mixture into two smaller sized pans if needed. They freeze well and last in the fridge for at least two weeks. Warning, they are addictive! *Adapted from dietdoctor.com.*

INGREDIENTS

1/3 cup raw sunflower seeds
1/3 cup whole flax seeds
1/3 cup almond flour
1/3 cup raw sesame seeds
1/3 cup raw pumpkin seeds
1 tbsp psyllium husk powder
1 tsp sea salt
1 tsp garlic powder
1 tsp onion powder
½ tsp ground cumin
2 tbsp olive oil
1 cup boiling water

METHOD

1. Preheat oven to 300° Farenheit.

2. Put the kettle on to the boil water. While the water is heating add all of your dry ingredients into a bowl. Add your oil and one cup of boiling water and mix together. Let sit for about 30 seconds, you may feel it is too much water but the psyllium will soak it up.

3. Spread the mixture onto a large baking sheet (16x12) lined with parchment paper. Be sure to spread it to the edges of the baking sheet to ensure a thin cracker. Bake for about 45 minutes, until the whole cracker sheet is lightly browned and crispy. Remove from the oven and let sit until cool. Break into pieces and eat with avocado, cheese, chimichurri, cashew dip etc.

Seedy Gluten-Free Bread

DAIRY FREE, GLUTEN FREE, GRAIN FREE + NUT FREE | YIELD 12–14 SLICES

THIS IS MOM'S BREAD, SHE loves it and I love her. It's super easy to make and in my opinion, it tastes really good and freezes really well.

INGREDIENTS

1 cup arrowroot flour
4 tbsp coconut flour
2 tsp baking powder
1 tsp baking soda
1 tsp salt
1 tbsp psyllium husk powder
3 tbsp flax meal
2 tbsp chia seeds
4 tbsp pumpkin seeds
2 tbsp sesame seeds
¾ cup zucchini (peeled and shredded)
4 eggs
¼ cup apple sauce
4 tbsp olive oil
Topping: sprinkle chia + pumpkin seeds on top

METHOD

1. Preheat oven 325°F.

2. Combine dry ingredients in a bowl and wet ingredients in another bowl and whisk wet ingredients together.

3. Add the dry to the wet, fold together with a spatula. Add the batter to a greased loaf pan and bake for 40-45 minutes. Pierce with a wooden skewer to check for doneness.

Note: This bread should be toasted or warmed in the oven after the first day to bring back the soft moist texture.

Soups

Soups can actually be an amazingly nutrient dense meal any time of the day. One of my awesome clients told me she mostly eats soup for her breakfast in the winter months, and I think this is a great idea! It emanates calmness at the beginning of the day and prevents you from rushing out the door. Add diced avocado and a tablespoon of cold pressed olive oil to your warm soup for extra good fat.

All of my soups are made with homemade bone broth, as you get the best flavour when you roast your bones first to get them brown and crispy. I love using an insta pot to make a quick broth after roasting the bones because it normally takes 8 to 24 hours to make a beautiful flavourful broth on the stove, whereas the insta pot takes just one and half hours. My go-to ingredients for broth are carrots, celery, leek tops, onion, fennel and bay leaf.

Quick Immune Cup of Soup

DAIRY FREE, GLUTEN FREE, GRAIN FREE | YIELD 8–10 CUPS

YOU CAN ADD SUMMER POTATOES to this soup as well as cooked rice or butternut squash. I love the simplicity of this beautiful nourishing and simple soup. Whenever I am sick I go towards this soup because the leeks feed my gut bacteria and the broth helps heal my gut lining. It's easy to digest and does not take all of my energy away from healing.

INGREDIENTS

1 cup leeks (chopped)
1 garlic clove (minced)
2 tsp butter
1½ cups homemade chicken or beef bone broth
⅛ tsp chili flakes
Salt and pepper

METHOD

1. In a small soup pot heat your butter and add your leeks and sprinkle with salt and pepper. Cover and allow the leeks to soften for about two to three minutes.

2. Remove the lid and add your garlic and chili flakes, sauté for about one minute. Add your broth and simmer for about 10 minutes.

Chicken Bone Broth Soup

DAIRY FREE, GLUTEN FREE, GRAIN FREE | YIELD 10–12 CUPS

I MEAN, IT'S A CLASSIC and this is my version, and the dill is the love in this recipe.

INGREDIENTS

2-3 cups cooked organic free-range chicken (cubed or shredded)

3 cups white cabbage (chopped small)

1½ cups onion (diced small)

2 cups carrot (sliced thin)

¼ cup fresh dill (chopped)

10 cups homemade chicken or beef bone broth

¼ cup olive oil

METHOD

1. Heat a large soup pot on low/medium heat, add the olive oil and onions. Sautee the onions for five minutes until translucent, then add the carrots and bone broth.

2. Cover and bring to a simmer. Once simmering, add the chopped cabbage and simmer for about 10 minutes more. Remove from the stove and add the chicken, freshly chopped dill. Season with salt and pepper.

Kale + Lentil Soup

DAIRY FREE, GLUTEN FREE, GRAIN FREE | YIELD 8–10 CUPS

THE BEEF BONE BROTH IN this soup is key if you ask me, it adds a richness that just coats your tongue with rooting flavours. It feels nourishing and cozy in your belly and the lemon at the end encapsulates all of the flavours and makes it perfect.

INGREDIENTS

1 cup green lentils (soaked for 30 minutes)
2 cups carrots (diced small)
2 cups onion (diced small)
1 cup leeks (chopped medium)
1 cup celery (diced small)
1 tsp fresh thyme or 1/2 teaspoon dry
1 tsp chilli flakes
1½ tsp garlic (minced)
3 tbsp tomato paste
8 cups homemade beef broth (page 75)
3 cups cabbage
4 tbsp olive oil or butter
3 cups kale
½ to 1 lemon (squeezed over soup after it is ready)
Salt and pepper to taste

METHOD

1. Soak your lentils in water for about 30 minutes prior to cooking. If you cannot do this step just rinse them and know the soup will take a little longer to cook.

2. Heat your olive oil up in a large soup pot and add the onions and leek, sauté them for a couple of minutes before adding your garlic, celery, carrots, thyme and chilli flakes.

3. Sauté the vegetables for two to three minutes before adding the remainder of the ingredients except for the kale and lemon juice. Cover and simmer for about 10-15 minutes. Remove from heat and add your kale and lemon juice to taste. Season with salt and pepper.

Chicken or Beef Bonebroth

DAIRY FREE, GLUTEN FREE, GRAIN FREE | YIELD 10–12 CUPS

THERE IS NOTHING MORE NOURISHING and tasty than homemade bone broth. Once I started making my own broth I honestly never went back. Soup just didn't taste or feel the same in my body. I use my 8 quart insta pot to make my broth in 90 minutes. The key to an amazing deep and rich tasting broth is roasting your bones first, if you can't do this, don't worry, it's just great that you are trying to make your own. If you can't make your own, no problem, there are many amazing frozen broths out there. When you think bone broth think gut healing.

INGREDIENTS

1400 grams beef bones
or two chicken carcasses
2-3 large carrots
2 large onions
½ fennel bulb
3 bay leaves
3 stalks celery
The green tops of 1-2 leeks
Cold water

***NOTE:** if using a smaller insta pot, divide the recipe in about half. Skim the fat off the top of the broth once strained and cooled.

METHOD

1. Roast your bones on a baking sheet at 400°F for 20-25 minutes or until they get browned and crispy. Deglaze your baking sheet with water and get all those crispy bits off the pan and add the liquid to your pot.

2. Add all of your ingredients to your *8 quart insta pot or large stock pot and cover the bones and veggies with COLD water. Don't add too much water, you want just enough to cover the bones by an extra two inches or so.

3. Place the lid on the insta pot and pressure cook for 1.5 hours. Let slow release for 10 minutes and then strain. If you are using the stove top, you will want to cover the stock pot with a lid and SLOWLY simmer that baby for at least 8 hours or use your crockpot for 24 hours.

Borscht with Sausage + Dill

DAIRY FREE, GLUTEN FREE, GRAIN FREE | YIELD 10–12 CUPS

I AM OBSESSED with this soup in the fall and winter. It doesn't taste as good if you leave the sausage out but if you must, go ahead but don't hate me if you're like, meh, the soup is just aiiight. It NEEDS the sausage dammit.

INGREDIENTS

2 tbsp olive oil

4 cups red cabbage (chopped medium)

2 cups carrots (chopped medium)

2 cups onions (chopped medium)

2 cups beets (chopped medium)

3 garlic cloves (minced)

450g pork sausage (casings removed, cut small)

2 tbsp tomato paste

½ tsp chilli flakes

7-8 cups homemade beef bone broth

½ cup fresh dill (chopped)

1-2 tbsp raw apple cider vinegar

Salt and pepper to taste

METHOD

1. Heat a large soup pot on medium heat and add the olive oil. Add your sausage in batches and cook until browned. Remove all the sausage from the pot and set aside in a bowl.

2. Add the onion and garlic to the same pot you cooked the sausage in, as the fat from the sausage will add flavour. Sauté the onion and garlic for a couple of minutes, then add the remainder of the vegetables. Sauté for 1-2 minutes longer and add the rest of your ingredients except for the sausage and dill, these will be added once removed from the stove.

3. Bring the soup to a simmer and cook for 15-20 minutes or until vegetables are done to your liking. Remove from the stove, add the fresh dill and sausage and season if needed. If you have healthy beet greens left over, chop these babies up and add them at the end!

Salads and Dressings

Salads are my go to in order to get my vegetables in, especially in the summer. I usually make two different salads a week and add my protein to them. They're the largest thing on my plate and I try to focus on what is seasonal.

All salads can be enjoyed with quality protein such as boiled pasture-raised eggs, grass-fed beef, pasture-raised chicken, beans, lentils, wild salmon or organic tofu.

Sesame Dressing

DAIRY FREE, GLUTEN FREE + VEGAN | YIELD ½ CUP

NEED SOME UMAMI IN YOUR LIFE? This dressing is super easy to whip up and you can use it with fresh local greens, but also drizzled over sautéed cabbage or as a marinade for meats.

INGREDIENTS

¼ cup toasted sesame oil

1 tbsp maple syrup

3 tbsp gluten-free tamari (light version)

3 tbsp balsamic vinegar

1 tsp fresh ginger (minced)

¼ teaspoon cayenne pepper

METHOD

1. Add everything to a mason jar and shake it up.

Flax + Turmeric Dressing

DAIRY FREE, GLUTEN FREE + VEGAN | YIELD 1 CUP

STORE BOUGHT SALAD DRESSINGS often really irritate me as most are super bad for you. They contain terrible quality vegetable oils, preservatives and a shit load of sugar. There is no need to purchase salad dressing. Do you want to coat your body with nutrients, anti-inflammatory compounds, and liver-loving ingredients? This dressing is a must, it is actually a healthy dressing that you can add more of, not less.

INGREDIENTS

¼ cup organic extra virgin olive oil
¼ cup organic flax oil
2 tsp organic Dijon mustard
2 tsp raw, local honey (omit for keto or vegan)
1 tsp fresh grated turmeric (or 1/4 tsp dry)
2 tbsp raw apple cider vinegar
2 tbsp organic gluten free "light" tamari (use less if not "light")
2 tsp garlic (minced)
Sea salt and pepper

METHOD

1. Add everything to a mason jar and either shake it up or blend with a hand blender. BOOM!

Note: This is a staple salad dressing in my house. It's delicious on salad, obviously, but also on avocado toasts and drizzled over cherry tomatoes.

Lemon Dressing

DAIRY FREE, GLUTEN FREE + VEGAN | YIELD 1 CUP

ONE OF MY FAVOURITES, this is a light tasty dressing that goes with just about every salad. The onion powder and lemon zest are the love in this recipe for sure. I like to use this dressing to coat my cabbage slaw that goes with my taco bowl.

INGREDIENTS

Zest of one lemon
½ tsp onion powder
2 tbsp Dijon mustard
¼ cup freshly squeezed lemon juice
2 tsp raw honey (omit if keto or vegan)
½ cup olive oil
¼ teaspoon sea salt and pepper

METHOD

1. Add everything to a mason jar and shake it up, it's that easy peezy!

Antioxidant Summer Salad

DAIRY FREE, GLUTEN FREE + VEGAN | YIELD 4 PORTIONS

SUMMER TIME IS FOR CRISP, fresh salads, and this one hits the spot. The best part is it can all be made in your food processor, which gives you more time to be at the beach with your family or wherever else you'd rather be than the kitchen! I really like adding some sesame grilled chicken, pan-fried scallops or salmon on top of this salad. It's a great salad to bring to work.

INGREDIENTS

1 cup carrot (shredded)

2 cups parsley (chopped)

3 cups red cabbage (shredded)

⅓ cup roasted pistachios or almonds

Lemon Dressing (page 85)

METHOD

1. In a medium sized mason jar, prepare the Lemon Dressing (page 85).

2. Shred the carrots and red cabbage with a food processor, chop by hand or use a grater. Add all chopped or shredded ingredients to a large bowl and toss with desired amount of salad dressing.

Note: Always roast nuts at 300°F or less until lightly toasted. The salad will keep for a couple of days in an air tight container without dressing added.

Brussels Buster Salad

GLUTEN FREE + GRAIN FREE | YIELD 6–8 PORTIONS

WHO DOESN'T LIKE BRUSSELS? UM, yes many people don't but, may I say, when you shred these babies you will develop a new love for them if you were a hater before. Your liver loves them as well so get over it and eat 'em!

INGREDIENTS

4 cups Brussels sprouts (shredded)
4 cups kale (chopped fine)
½ cup fresh blueberries or ripe pear
⅓ cup almonds (toasted lightly and chopped)
½ cup shaved Parmigiano Reggiano cheese
Lemon Dressing (page 85)

METHOD

1. In a medium sized mason jar, prepare the Lemon Dressing (page 85).

2. In a large bowl, toss together the shredded kale, shredded Brussels sprouts, cheese and toasted almonds. Add as much dressing as desired, tossing to combine, then sprinkle blueberries on top.

Note: This salad is great leftover the next day. You can also have all ingredients prepped ahead and keep them in the fridge for up to four days, just toss with dressing day of. I like to have to hard boiled eggs mashed on top of this salad or grilled filet mignon, oh yah!

Liver Lover Salad

GLUTEN FREE, GRAIN-FREE, NUT-FREE + VEGAN | 4 SMALL OR 2 LARGE SERVING

THIS SALAD IS SO DELICIOUS LEFTOVER and lasts in the fridge for three or four days. Our liver loves the bitter artichokes, nutrient dense chlorophyl in the parsley and sulphur containing raw garlic. If your liver is not optimal, you won't be optimal! Add four or five ounces of grilled fish or sausage on top of your salad and boom: complete meal!

INGREDIENTS

1 cup or 165 grams (10) artichoke hearts
3 cups fresh parsley (chopped)
2 tbsp capers
¼ cup raisins
½ cup cucumber (diced)
¼ cup red onion (small dice)
1 cup cooked red quinoa or millet
Zest and juice of 1 lemon
1 large garlic clove (minced)
3 tbsp olive oil
Salt and pepper to taste

METHOD

1. Lightly squeeze out the water from the artichokes and cut them into four, add them to a large bowl.

2. Add the rest of your ingredients to the bowl and toss together.

Note: Purchase artichokes in a glass jar with water and squeeze lightly to eliminate liquid.

Herby Asian Salad

DAIRY FREE, GLUTEN FREE + VEGAN | YIELD 6–8 SERVINGS

HERBS IN GENERAL ARE SO under appreciated; they can feed your body with high quality nutrients and give so many boring dishes a boost of flavour. This is my dad's favourite recipe and he continues to lose the recipe and has to ask me to send it to him on a monthly basis. I mean, I'm not annoyed or anything, just sayin'.

INGREDIENTS

3 cups red cabbage (sliced thin, use food processor)
1½ cups or 1 bunch green onion (sliced thin on an angle)
1½ cups red pepper (sliced thin on an angle)
2 cups snap peas (sliced thin on an angle)
1½ cups or 1 bunch cilantro (chopped coarsely)
1 cup mint (chopped coarsely)
1 cup basil (chopped coarsely)
1-2 cups cooked and chopped rice noodles (optional)
Sesame Dressing (page 81)

METHOD

1. I like to double this recipe. Prepare the Sesame Dressing (page 81) in a mason jar and shake up.

2. Slice all of your ingredients and add them to a large bowl.

3. When you are ready to eat toss with your sesame salad dressing and enjoy with grilled shrimp, chicken, portobellos or your choice of protein.

Note: I toss my rice noodles in sesame oil after they are cooked.

Mains

I am actually not a traditional meal kind of girl. Shocking right? I make a meal around what I have in the fridge, what staples I have prepared ahead of time and then build a meal around that. I have made these traditional 'mains' as my sides. I want to start encouraging you to think that the meat or plant based protein part of your meal is the side not the main. Cheeky right?

Mexican Shepherds Pie

GLUTEN FREE, GRAIN FREE, NUT FREE | YIELD 4 PORTIONS

WHEN PEOPLE TASTE THIS, FROWNS turn upside down. No shit! It freezes super well and even kids love it. I love it because I use a cauliflower and sweet potato topping and people don't even realize they are eating nutrient dense cauliflower instead of regular potato.

INGREDIENTS

2½ cups sweet potato
2½ cups cauliflower
1 lb organic ground beef, pork or turkey
1 cup onion
1 large garlic clove
1 tbsp chipotle in adobo sauce
1 tsp oregano
1 tbsp chili powder
½ tsp cumin
2 tsp Montreal steak spice
¼ tsp cinnamon
¼ cup diced tomatoes
1½ tbsp tomato paste
⅓ cup water
1 tbsp coconut oil
½ cup grated organic grass-fed gouda (optional)
¼ cup chopped cilantro
Juice from one lime

METHOD

1. Steam the sweet potato and cauliflower separately until soft. Mash cauliflower with hand blender or food processor and sweet potato by hand, then fold together. Season with salt and pepper and 1 tablespoon of butter or coconut oil or olive oil.

2. In a large skillet, cook the onions in the coconut oil until translucent, add the garlic, then the beef and brown. Add your spices and cook for another minute.

3. Add the rest of your ingredients except for the cheese, lime and cilantro. I like to simmer the mixture covered for about 15 minutes, then I take the lid off and reduce the liquid until it looks delish, ha!

4. Remove from heat and add the lime juice and cilantro. Add meat to a pyrex dish, then the cheese and the mash on top. Bake at 350 ° F until hot and bubbly.

5. Serve with sour cream, Authentic Guacamole and Pico de Gallo Salsa.

Beef Taco Cabbage Bowl

DAIRY FREE, GLUTEN FREE + GRAIN FREE | YIELD 4–6 PORTIONS

THIS IS A QUICK GO-TO in my house during the spring and summer. I make a double batch of the meat mixture and serve it in different ways during the week. The cabbage slaw lasts about a week in the fridge without adding the lime juice so it's very handy to have on hand.

INGREDIENTS

1 tbsp coconut oil
1 cup onions (chopped)
2 cloves garlic (minced)
1 lb organic ground beef or pork
3 tbsp tomato paste
1 tbsp chili powder
1 tsp cumin
⅛ tsp cloves
2 tsp oregano
¼ tsp cinnamon
½ to ¾ tsp sea salt
½ tsp chili flakes
1 tsp honey
¾ cup water
1 lime
½ cup cilantro (chopped, added at the end)
Salt and pepper to taste

SLAW
4 to 6 cups cabbage (shredded)
1 cup carrots (shredded)
Fresh lime juice or Lemon Dressing (page 85)

METHOD

1. In a medium sized frying pan, heat the coconut oil to medium heat and add your onions. Sauté the onions for five to ten minutes then add the minced garlic and cook for another minute or so. Add your ground beef and brown, then add the tomato paste and spices and sauté until fully cooked.

2. Add the water and simmer on low/medium heat, covered for about 12 minutes. After 12 minutes remove the lid and simmer for another 15 minutes until some of the liquid has evaporated. Reserve a little liquid to smother the slaw with.

3. Remove from the stove, squeeze fresh lime juice over the ground beef mixture and the chopped cilantro, season with fresh pepper and sea salt.

4. Toss your cabbage slaw with my lemon dressing or just straight up lime juice and olive oil or a creamy coleslaw dressing.

5. Serve warm taco meat on top of the slaw, add your toppings of choice such as sour cream, shredded cheese, Authentic Guacamole and Pico de Gallo Salsa.

I made this with skinless chicken thighs, cooked them for about 45 minutes flipping them over once and dammmmmn, they taste like the most delicious fried chicken ever.

If you want to freeze these babies, freeze them uncooked. When cooking from frozen, bake for 25-30 minutes.

Crispy Chicken Tenders

DAIRY FREE, GLUTEN FREE + NUT FREE | YIELD 12–14 TENDERS

WHO DOESN'T LIKE chicken tenders? Most chicken tenders are coated in inflammatory oils, gluten breadcrumbs and preservatives. These babies are alllllll good in the hood. They freeze super well and you can make a whole bunch and have them ready when you're on the go. Efficient right?

INGREDIENTS

615 grams chicken breast (cut into 12-14 tenders)
1 cup sweet rice flour
2 tbsp flax meal
1 tbsp garlic powder
1 tbsp onion powder
½ tsp cayenne
1¼ tsp salt
1 tbsp chili powder
¼ cup coconut milk
2 eggs
Olive oil for baking

METHOD

1. Cut up your chicken breast into tenders. Combine the dry ingredients in a large bowl and set aside. Mix the eggs and coconut milk together in another bowl.

2. Here is the important technique to make these super crispy and delish: dredge the chicken tenders in the flour mixture and then in the egg mixture and finally one last time in the flour mixture. Be sure not to overcrowd your baking sheet or frying pan when cooking them.

3. You have two ways of cooking these babies up:

A: Pan fry them with a generous amount of olive oil or coconut oil, being cautious not to overcrowd the pan so they crisp up evenly on each side.

B: Line a baking sheet with parchment paper, grease it with olive oil, place the chicken tenders on the oiled parchment paper being sure not to overcrowd, then drizzle more olive oil and bake 400°F for 15 minutes. After 15 minutes, flip each one over and bake for another 10-14 minutes.

Serve with Tzaziki Sauce (page 107) and a big-ass salad.

I was inspired by a friend I met in Cabo San Lucas when I was living there. She was originally from Israel and one time she made this amazing beef dish with dried fruit and nuts and I thought to myself, oh God I'm going to have to get some tacos after this because how can dried fruit and nuts taste good simmered with meat? Um, fully humbled that day, I was wrong and I admit it!

Moroccan-Style Chicken

DAIRY FREE, GLUTEN FREE + GRAIN FREE | YIELD 4–6 PORTIONS

NOBODY LOVES THIS CHICKEN MORE than my mom because it has a little bit of sweetness to it. Use boneless chicken thighs, skin on for flavour or off if you are boring. Your choice, no judgment.

INGREDIENTS

4 (1lb) chicken thighs, skin on
2 (1lb) chicken breast
(cut into 2-3 large pieces)
21/4 cups onions (sliced)
Salt and pepper for seasoning
2 tbsp garlic (minced)
2 tbsp olive oil, ghee or butter
2/3 cup raw cashews
1/2 cup raw almonds
6-8 dates (seeded and chopped medium)
1/3 cup raisins
2 cups water
11/2 tbsp tapioca +11/2 tbsp water
1/2 cup cilantro
Juice of 1/2 lemon

METHOD

1. Season chicken pieces with a generous amount of salt and pepper. Heat the oil of choice on medium in a large frying pan and brown chicken pieces in batches. Place the chicken into a large braising dish and set aside.

2. Next add the onions to the same frying pan, straight into the warm fat from the chicken... that's where the flavour starts to build up.

3. Pan fry the onions until browned, then add the garlic, nuts, dates and raisins. If you need to add a little more oil at this point go ahead. Pan fry the whole mixture for another five to eight minutes just to bring all of the flavours together.

4. Add two cups of water to deglaze the pan and then add that mixture to your braising dish containing the chicken, which will get bathed in all that deliciousness.

5. Season with salt and pepper, cover and simmer on low heat for about 40 minutes or until chicken is very tender. Once the chicken has tenderized, remove the lid and increase the heat to a light boil. Mix the tapioca starch and water together and stir it into the chicken, it will thicken quickly. Remove from heat, add cilantro and lemon and season more if needed.

Dips and Sauces

Dips and sauces are great flavour boosters that can contain powerful nutrients and pack a tasty punch. I always have one or two dips or flavour boosters in my fridge, they are so much better than conventional condiments that are usually filled with sugar, GMO and preservatives.

Super Yummy Tzaziki Sauce

GLUTEN-FREE + GRAIN-FREE | YIELD 2 CUPS

TZAZIKI SAUCE CAN BE A nutrient dense flavour booster if you choose to use quality ingredients. Choose organic grass-fed yogurt and sour cream, use fresh dill and fresh garlic. These powerful ingredients can help boost your gut health and detoxification system.

INGREDIENTS

1 cup plain organic grass-fed yogurt
1/2 cup sour cream
1/4 cup sheep feta
1/4 cup red onion (diced small)
1 tbsp garlic (minced)
1/3 cup fresh dill
2/3 cup cucumber (grated and squeeze water out)
Juice of one lemon
1/2 teaspoon salt
Pepper to taste

METHOD

1. Add everything to a bowl, stir together and serve over grilled chicken, salmon, vegetables or whatever your heart desires.

Muhamarra Dip

DAIRY FREE, GLUTEN FREE, GRAIN FREE + VEGAN | YIELD 2 CUPS

THIS DIP IS SO DELICIOUS with raw crudité, or used as a spread on top of your roasted, grilled fish or meat. You can also use this dip as a sandwich or burger spread ... oh and warning, it's addictive, but in a good way!

INGREDIENTS

1½ cups organic walnuts (lightly roasted)
12 oz. jar of roasted red peppers, drained
3 tbsp extra virgin olive oil
2 large garlic cloves
1 tbsp onion
½ tsp ground cumin
1 tsp dried chili flakes
Sea salt and fresh pepper to taste

METHOD

1. Combine all ingredients in a food processor and pulse until smooth, then season with sea salt and pepper.

Note: 'Lightly roasted' means roast your nuts at 300° F for 5-10 minutes.

Chimichurri Sauce

DAIRY FREE, GLUTEN FREE, GRAIN FREE + VEGAN | YIELD 11/2 CUPS

THIS SUPER HIGH ANTIOXIDANT dip is delicious on everything, for real! It's important to use high quality organic cold pressed olive oil because you are using a lot of it and it will coat all of your cells with the proper fat they need. Whatever you grill this summer, add this to your veggies or meat after they have been cooked and you will love me a little bit more :)

INGREDIENTS

1 bunch Italian parsley

½ bunch cilantro

¼ cup onion

1 tsp dried chili flakes

1 tsp dried oregano (1 tbsp fresh)

2-3 cloves garlic

2 tbsp red wine vinegar

½ cup to 1 cup extra virgin organic olive oil

Sea salt and fresh ground pepper

¼ to ½ cup extra virgin organic olive oil (for the top)

METHOD

1. In a food processor add your garlic and onion, pulse two or three times.

2. Add your fresh herbs, spices, the vinegar and three tablespoons of the olive oil and pulse a couple more times until you get your desired consistency.

3. Pour the chimichurri into a glass storage container and stir in the rest of the olive oil.

Note: You want the chimichurri to have a coating of olive oil on top, so if you need to add a little more olive oil, do so. This preserves the chimichurri and allows it to sit in the fridge for weeks, you can even freeze it in little ice cube trays if you like.

Snacks

Snacks are optional, I usually do not recommend snacking too much in between meals, your body needs that time (about four hours) to digest properly, allow the small intestine to empty fully and to absorb nutrients from your last meal. By snacking often you are never giving your body a rest from insulin. With that said I usually eat something at about 4pm while I am preparing dinner and if having healthy snacks can prevent you going through a drive through window, that's always a good thing.

Tia's Super Awesome Elixir

DAIRY FREE, GLUTEN FREE, + GRAIN FREE | YIELD 24 CUPS

THIS BEAUTIFUL BABY was created on a cold grey night on Vancouver Island as I was thinking of what foods are warming, nutrient dense, efficient, soothing and healing. Please use real raw cacao powder for this, not cocoa powder that is dutch processed.

INGREDIENTS

ELIXIR MIX

80 grams / 1 cup raw cacao

8 grams / 2 tsp sea salt

24 grams / 4 tbsp cinnamon

8 grams / 4 tsp turmeric

16 grams / 4 tbsp ginger

3 grams / 2 tsp pepper

TO SERVE

5 grams of elixir / 1 tbsp

1 tsp raw honey

1 tsp vanilla extract

1 cup coconut mylk or other nut mylk

METHOD

1. Combine all the elixir ingredients into a large bowl and whisk together, place the deliciousness into a mason jar.

2. Add 1 tbsp elixir mix to a pot, then add the honey, vanilla extract and mylk. Stir over low heat to combine and warm.

The Trendy Avocado Toast

DAIRY FREE, GLUTEN FREE + GRAIN FREE | YIELD 1 PORTION

YES I DECIDED TO ADD the most trendy snack of the 21st century to my book (eyes rolling). It really is a super easy, nutrient-dense snack or breakfast or lunch or for whatever-time-of-day you want. But, I do want to make you aware that the more we demand foods like avocados the harder it is for the people who grow them. There are literally avocado wars out there where cartels have taken over people's farms. Please be aware of trendy food and try to consume less of these foods if possible.

INGREDIENTS

2 slices of Seedy Nut Bread (page 65)
½ ripe avocado (mashed with a fork)
2 tbsp of Flax/Turmeric salad dressing (page 83)
Sheep Feta (optional)

METHOD

1. You can toast your nut bread a little in the toaster oven or not.

2. Divide the mashed avocado on to the slices of nut bread and drizzle with the flax and turmeric salad dressing.

Brazil Nut Trail Mix

DAIRY FREE, GLUTEN FREE, GRAIN FREE + VEGAN | YIELD 6 PORTIONS

THE BEST WAY TO GET your selenium is eating two to four brazil nuts a day. Selenium is necessary for proper liver detoxification and our immune health depends on it.

INGREDIENTS

12 Brazil nuts

¼ cup raw cacao nibs

¼ cup dried gogi berries

¼ cup raw pumpkin seeds

METHOD

1. Toss all of your delicious nutrient dense ingredients together and eat a handful a day. Be sure to include two brazil nuts a day for selenium.

A Bit of Real Sweetness

We all need a little bit of sweetness in our lives but we do not have to get it from refined, highly processed sources or even large amounts of natural sweeteners. It is amazing what mother nature has created for us when it comes to adding a little bit of sweetness to our food plan. All of the below recipes have very little sugar added if any, so your taste buds may take a little while to adjust. Give it time and you may learn to have a new appreciation for a little bit of sweetness.

Homemade Apple Sauce

GLUTEN FREE, GRAIN FREE, NUT FREE + VEGAN | YIELD 2 CUPS

APPLE SAUCE IS A STAPLE in my house. It is so versatile, I always make sure to have some in my refrigerator and freezer.

INGREDIENTS

8 cups Ambrosia or Gala apples (chopped, skin on)

2 tbsp olive oil

1 tsp Ceylon cinnamon

METHOD

1. Add all of your ingredients to a medium pot, place on low heat with the lid on.
2. Simmer for about 20 minutes while occasionally stirring.
3. Remove from heat, blend it up and BOOM! Let it cool and then place it in the fridge or freezer.

Oh Snap!

Studies show consuming pectin from plant sources like apples helps reduce intestinal inflammation caused by powerful endotoxins such as as lipopolysaccharide (LPS). Consume two tablespoons of homemade apple sauce a day to keep the doctor away! [14]

Better Coconut Mylk

GLUTEN FREE, GRAIN FREE, NUT FREE + VEGAN | YIELD 4 CUPS

COCONUT MILK AND ALMOND MILK are staples in my kitchen, I like this version because it can be cheaper than buying a carton of nut milk and I can find cans of coconut milk that do not contain preservatives or emulsifiers such as guar gum or carrageenan. These additives have a tendency to upset a sensitive digestive system but not everyone has issues. Remember, the dose makes the poison. The drawback to not having these additives is the coconut milk will not be as smooth and creamy. It will still taste delicious but not look as pretty, so I go back and forth to not overwhelm my system with unnecessary additives.

INGREDIENTS

1 can full fat coconut mylk

3 cups cold water

1 tsp vanilla extract

METHOD

1. Add all ingredients to a blender, blend for two to five seconds.
2. Add to a glass jar and refrigerate.

Oh Snap!

Check out my website Honey and Vanilla for Homemade Almond Mylk. Once you taste it, you will never go back to boxed nut mylk!

Carrot Pineapple Cake Muffins

GLUTEN-FREE + GRAIN-FREE | YIELD 12 MUFFINS

I CREATED THESE BABIES BECAUSE my husband's birthday was coming up and his favorite dessert (well one of them) is carrot cake. He's weaning himself off of sugar overload so these muffins were the perfect creation to avoid excess sugar. They are super moist and won't disappoint in flavour. Be sure to have everything at room temperature and to sift the coconut flour, it does make a difference in texture in the end. Like many gluten-free desserts these freeze well but I would recommend heating them slightly to bring back their soft moist personalities.

INGREDIENTS

⅔ cup coconut flour
⅓ cup tapioca flour
1 tsp baking powder (aluminum free)
½ teaspoon baking soda (aluminum free)
1 tbsp true cinnamon
2 tsp ground ginger
¼ tsp salt
4 eggs (room temperature)
¼ cup coconut mylk (room temperature)
¼ cup butter (melted)
2 tbsp pineapple juice from the can
1 tsp almond extract + 2 tsp vanilla extract
2 tbsp raw honey
1 tbsp raw apple cider vinegar
2 cups carrot (shredded)
¼ cup pineapple chunks (canned)
¼ cup raisins

METHOD

1. Preheat oven to 350°F degrees.

2. In a medium bowl combine your eggs, butter and mylk, pineapple juice, almond and vanilla extract, apple cider vinegar and honey. Beat the wet ingredients with a hand beater or fork, just be sure to mix well. Add your raisin and pineapple chunks, set the bowl aside.

3. In another bowl combine dry ingredients; be sure to sift the coconut flour into the bowl. Add your dry ingredients to the wet and fold together until well combined. Spray your muffin tin with coconut or olive oil and divide the mixture into the pan. Bake for 18-20 minutes. You can slightly reheat these babies to ensure soft moistness after the first day, they also freeze well, just be sure to reheat.

Raw Cacao + Nut Butter Muffins

GLUTEN FREE, GRAIN FREE + VEGAN | YIELD 12 MUFFINS

NO ONE BELIEVES these are actually good for you. They call them cupcakes, not muffins. This is one of the recipes I am most proud of so far. They are sooooo good, soft, moist, freeze well and you don't have to feel guilty for eating them.

INGREDIENTS

1 cup pure cashew or peanut butter

1 cup banana

3 tbsp ground flax seeds

4 tablespoons water

¾ cup full-fat coconut mylk

¼ cup organic raw cacao powder

¼ tsp ACV (raw apple cider vinegar)

1 tsp baking powder (aluminum free)

¼ tsp sea salt

1 tsp vanilla extract

METHOD

1. Preheat oven to 350° F.

2. Combine your flax/water mixture in a small bowl and let stand in the fridge for 10 minutes.

3. Add your nut butter and bananas into a food processor and puree together until light and fluffy. This ensures fluffy moist chocolate babies.

4. Add the rest of your ingredients and mix until smooth.

5. Split the mixture into 12 muffin holders, (I use silicone molds, they pop out so easily). Bake at 350° F for 15-18 minutes.

Note: You don't want to over cook these! It may take a couple of times to perfect the doneness, but when you press your finger on top of the muffin, you want to see it bounce back a little.

Oh Snap!

I have found so many nut butter brands add sunflower or safflower oil to their butters, this is BS. Be sure to purchase your nut butters with no added oils unless it is organic olive oil or unrefined coconut oil.

Soft + Moist Chocolate Chip Cookies

DAIRY FREE, GLUTEN FREE, GRAIN FREE + VEGAN | YIELD 20 COOKIES

WHAT CAN I SAY ABOUT THESE amazingly delicious, soft, moist babies. They are delicious frozen, I know that's weird but I crave them cold. I was so happy to create a cookie recipe that didn't involve regular sugar, brown sugar or a ton of shortening. I do not feel bad about eating them and neither should you.

INGREDIENTS

2 medium ripe bananas (1 1/4 cups)
½ cup pumpkin puree
1/2 cup natural, salted peanut or almond butter
1 tbsp organic coconut oil, melted
1 tsp pure vanilla extract
1 tbsp maple syrup (optional)
21/4 cups almond meal
2 tbsp coconut flour (sifted)
1/2 teaspoon cinnamon
1/2 teaspoon baking powder
1/2 teaspoon baking soda
Pinch sea salt
1/3 cup pecans (chopped)
1/2 cup dairy free, gluten free semisweet or dark chocolate chips

METHOD

1. Preheat oven to 350°F degrees. Mash the bananas until well combined, and then add peanut butter, maple syrup, vanilla, coconut oil and pumpkin.

2. Add the rest of your ingredients and combine well.

3. Drop cookies by the spoonful or with a one ounce sized ice cream scoop onto a baking sheet lined with parchment paper. Push the cookies down a bit with a fork or your moistened fingers, as they will expand a little. Bake for 18-20 minutes or until the cookies are slightly golden brown. Let rest on baking sheet for a few minutes before transferring to a cooling rack.

Vanilla + Cardamom Chia

GLUTEN FREE, GRAIN FREE + VEGAN | YIELD 4 PORTIONS

BOWELS NOT WORKING OPTIMALLY? Try chia pudding. I eat this on a regular basis as a great dessert or part of a break-fast. No need for added sugar as the berries and banana (if you add them) add a perfect sweetness. Some people don't like the look or texture of chia pudding, but I say in the nicest way possible, "Get over it and expand your taste buds and mind."

INGREDIENTS

1½ cups coconut mylk (page 125w) **or homemade almond mylk**

1 tsp organic vanilla extract

¼ cup chia seeds

1 tsp Ceylon cinnamon

⅛ tsp ground cardamom (optional but delicious)

TOPPINGS:
berries, raw cacao nibs, raw sunflower seeds and raw pumpkin seeds

METHOD

1. Mix your coconut mylk, cinnamon, cardamom and vanilla together, then stir in your chia seeds until the chia has suspended itself in the coconut mylk (this just helps prevent clumping.)

2. Allow the mixture to thicken for three hours or over night. At times I add an extra ¼ cup of coconut mylk the next morning because it became too thick for my liking. Top with fresh or defrosted organic berries

Note: You can make this ahead and divide the pudding into small mason jars, add your fresh or defrosted berries and put them in the fridge for a quick dessert or breakfast for the week. For a twist, try the Chocolate Banana Chia Pudding found on my website.

JERUSALEM
PLENTY MORE
THE SILVER PALATE COOKBOOK
Healing with Whole Foods
Asian Traditions and Modern Nutrition

STOCKING YOUR PANTRY

Preferred Ingredients

Over the years I have questioned certain brands and their ingredients. I was shocked one day when I turned my container of organic grass-fed sour cream around and it contained "natural" thickeners and colorings. I also read the back of "healthy" nut butters and realized they contained safflower oil, WTF? This blew my mind and changed everything from that point on.

Below is a list of the products I use to ensure I am getting quality over quantity. The point of this list is to explain that just because the product says it's healthy and organic, it may not be good for you. You may think, "it's just mustard, it can't be bad for you," but you might be wrong. I am here to say don't judge a book by it's cover.

We all use many of the below products daily, so remember to choose the right ones as excess creates imbalance and accumulation over the years. All of these preferred ingredients are probably a little more pricey than what you are used to spending, but these small changes can help increase your optimal health, so replace what you can.

Ceylon Cinnamon — Has a more mild flavor than it's sister Saigon, which is also called cassia. Ceylon cinnamon has less of the fragrant compound coumarin and has been shown to have medicinal qualities, such as helping lower blood sugar levels. If you use Saigon cinnamon or cassia in my recipes instead, you may need to use less because it has a more pungent flavor and can over power the end result.

Baking Soda and Baking Powder (Aluminum-Free) — High amounts of aluminum in the body have been linked to Alzheimer's disease so I'm choosing aluminum-free all the way! I do find it doesn't last as long as the regular baking soda/powder but I date them when I get them home and use them up in about three months.

Raw Cacao — Many people use cocoa powder instead of raw cacao powder. There is no comparison. If you are stranded on a desert island, cocoa powder is not going to get you anywhere. Raw cacao powder will keep you strong and healthy for a long time. Look for fair trade, organic raw cacao powder, it's worth the investment.

Canned Foods — Look for canned foods that say BPA free, Iike Eden brand. They use a type of tree resin to line their cans and I believe they use seaweed to preserve.

Mayonnaise — I mean who doesn't like mainstream mayo? But if you care about your health you will cut down on it and start making your own with extra virgin olive oil or use a product like Primal Kitchen mayo that uses avocado oil.

Olive Oil — Look for organic, cold pressed extra virgin olive oil. If you want to be more adventurous, some high quality olive oils include a date on the back showing when the olives were pressed, an expiry date and the total amount of polyphenols. Don't buy "light" olive oil as it's been highly processed and will just increase inflammation in your body.

Dried Herbs and Spices — In general I purchase small amounts of organic dried herbs and spices from my local grocery store and fill up once used. I also choose to buy larger amounts of quality organic herbs and spices from Om Foods to save some money but I am sure to use them up within 4 to 6 months.

Sauerkraut — Purchase raw sauerkraut from the refrigerator. Canned sauerkraut does not contain the health benefits raw sauerkraut contains.

Apple Cider Vinegar — You want to purchase RAW apple cider vinegar that contains "the mother". This "mother" holds many medicinal benefits for your body.

Raw Honey — Do yourself and the rest of the world a favor and support your local honey makers. Yes, once you heat this it will reduce it's healing properties but there is no comparison to commercial pasteurized honey. We're all connected man.

Chocolate Chips — I like to purchase fair trade, gluten-free, dairy-free, nut-free chocolate chips. I like the Camino brand as well as Enjoy Life brand.

Sour Cream and Plain Yogurt — Try to find a sour cream and plain yogurt that comes from organic grass-fed cows and that do not contain any thickeners such as carrageenan. I like Organic Meadows. If I can't find good quality organic sour cream or yogurt then I choose to buy non-organic that doesn't have any fillers or dyes or thickeners.

Vanilla Extract — Look for brands that say PURE organic vanilla extract or just PURE vanilla extract. Most brands contain food colouring, preservatives or artificial flavors. There should only be alcohol and vanilla bean in a quality extract. I like Simply Organic brand or if you do not want to spend more money you can find PURE vanilla extract from a brand like Clubhouse.

Salt — For now, I choose to go for Redmond Real Salt. Many salts contain anti-caking agents and studies are finding that most salts, especially sea salts, contain tiny little plastic particles because humans like to pollute the oceans with the stuff. Not cool. I do love using Maldon sea salt for salads and finishing dishes, so yes I just contradicted myself. But, with that said, 95% of the time I use Redmon Real Salt that comes from a mine.

Jarred Olives, Peppers, Pickles and Condiments — So many glass jarred products contain bad oils, preservatives such as sodium benzoate, and food colourings. Next time you purchase these products, read the labels. Look for products that say preserved in salt water, packed in olive oil, or raw pickles. I recall looking for a quality horseradish and I couldn't find one brand that didn't contain terrible additives until I found Bubbies brand.

Meat and Cheese — If you can purchase meat and cheese from a local farmer who believes in grass-fed only, organic or spray-free farming practices, you are doing you and your loved ones a huge favor. Yes it is usually more expensive but I believe we should be eating less of this anyway so when you do eat it why not go for the gold.

Parchment Paper and Foil — I like to use non-bleached parchment paper just as a precaution. I can't find any studies on whether bleached parchment paper is toxic, but I'm not going to take any chances.

Saran Wrap Alternative — I use beeswax sheets to cover my leftovers or use glass containers.

Gluten-Free Flour Alternatives — All of the following I try to buy organic: coconut flour, arrowroot flour, tapioca flour, cassava flour, almond flour, sweet rice flour, Bob's Redmill 1 to 1 baking flour. These are the flours I use instead of flours containing gluten.

Endnotes

1 https://www.who.int/features/factfiles/dementia/en/

2 https://www.ncbi.nlm.nih.gov/pmc/articles/PMC4221920/

3 https://www.ncbi.nlm.nih.gov/pmc/articles/PMC4703222/

4 https://podcasts.apple.com/dk/podcast/18-uncovering-hidden-causes-your-symptoms-dr-tom-obryan/id1381257272?i=1000418836020

5 https://health.gov/sites/default/files/2019-09/2015-2020_Dietary_Guidelines.pdf

6 https://health.gov/sites/default/files/2019-09/2015-2020_Dietary_Guidelines.pdf

7 https://www.who.int/publications/i/item/9789241549028

8 https://www.independent.co.uk/life-style/health-and-families/the-shockingly-small-amount-of-sugar-were-meant-to-eat-per-day-but-how-much-are-you-consuming-10087920.html

9 https://www.ncbi.nlm.nih.gov/pmc/articles/PMC1931610/

10 https://www.ketogenic-diet-resource.com/usda-food-pyramid.html

11 https://www.theguardian.com/society/2003/apr/21/usnews.food

12 https://www.who.int/nutrition/topics/2_background/en/

13 https://pubmed.ncbi.nlm.nih.gov/29754952/

14 https://www.cell.com/cell-metabolism/fulltext/S1550-4131(18)30253-5?_returnURL=https://linkinghub.elsevier.com/retrieve/pii/S1550413118302535?showall=true

15 https://www.sciencedaily.com/releases/2018/08/180831130131.htm

About the Author

CHRISTINA ACEVEDO WAS BORN and raised off of the island of Montreal, Quebec. She began her career back in Montreal where she received her Red Seal as a French Cuisine Chef. In 2006 she graduated as a Registered Holistic Nutritionist and created her business Honey and Vanilla. She has been a personal chef to movie stars in L.A, nourished children with autism, cooked for busy families and for many people with specific dietary needs.

She continues to advance her education by attending functional medicine webinars and conferences on preventing Alzheimer's, circadian rhythm, optimal health and fasting protocols. In 2018 she received a certification on the Fasting Mimicking Diet from Prolon at the University of Southern California, and in April 2020 received a certificate for attending a webinar on mold and mycotoxins.

Christina now lives on Vancouver Island in the middle of the forest with her husband. She strives to continue creating delicious whole food recipes while guiding you towards your optimal health through holistic living.

Contact her at www.HoneyandVanilla.com/contact

Follow her on Instagram at https://www.instagram.com/honeyandvanilla/

Made in the USA
Monee, IL
06 September 2021

76804426R00086